THE
Archive Photographs
SERIES

BAWTRY, TICKHILL AND WADWORTH

A scene outside a three storey building, traditionally known as the first house in Yorkshire, or No. 1 Yorkshire, when entering Bawtry from the south. The property is presently No. 2 South Parade and dates from the early nineteenth century. Unfortunately, none of the individuals depicted can be identified.

THE

Archive Photographs

SERIES

BAWTRY, TICKHILL AND WADWORTH

Compiled by

Peter Tuffrey

First published 1996

The Chalford Publishing Company
St Mary's Mill, Chalford,
Stroud, Gloucestershire, GL6 8NX

ISBN 0 7524 0623 X

Typesetting and origination by
The Chalford Publishing Company
Printed in Great Britain by
Redwood Books, Trowbridge

Patriotic Wadworth children, celebrating Empire Day 1912, are pictured outside the village's White Hart Inn when Henry Surr was the landlord.

Contents

For my good friend
George Read,
who was still smiling right to the end.

Introduction

The photographs in this volume are mostly reproduced from postcard views, dating from between 1905 to 1930. A large number were taken by just two photographers: Edgar Leonard Scrivens and George Crossland. Scrivens, based in Doncaster, was a professional photographer, taking literally thousands of pictures within a 50 mile radius of the town. His subjects were numerous and pictures cleverly composed, and always well populated, invariably with a group of children unashamedly posing in the foreground. Crossland, by comparison, rarely ventured outside Tickhill taking photographs. But, perhaps he did not have time as, like many businessmen of the period, he was deeply involved, for a number of years, with public life, being a JP and Chairman of the Tickhill Urban District Council.

Crossland's pictures are noted by their 'spidery' lettered captions, and his 'Feeding the Ducks' photograph at the outset of the Rambling Round section is a marvellous picture, that any well known professional would be proud of. It is interesting to note the children's style of dress and the design of the pram. But, perhaps what is most interesting to note, is that feeding the ducks is an activity still undertaken by children in the same area now. At the beginning of the section, we notice that Bawtry High Street/Market Place was once quite open, even roomy, not being a busy thoroughfare congested with motor vehicles as it is today. We are seeing the area after the demise of the coaching era and the heyday of the railways, giving way to the upsurge in motorised traffic. Hence the appearance, in the later pictures of the area, of roadside cafes and garages. The views of the other Bawtry streets, off the main highway, show buildings and houses in their unaltered and original condition, not spoilt by unsympathetic alterations and additions that we see today. I have included quite a number of Scrivens' Bawtry pictures (noted by his inscription ELS) in the Rambling section, particularly admiring those on pages 19, 24 and 25. The man with the white beard in the picture on page 24 looks to be a wonderful character and I would dearly like to know what occupation he held.

TheTickhill pictures also show the area uncluttered with traffic, though the one on page 32 shows that buildings were being altered unsympathetically even in those days. The bay windows added to one of the cottages look extremely unsightly. However, we are viewing Tickhill in the days when, I suspect most people worked within the area, unlike today because it is a dormitory village, some residents travelling great distances to their jobs. During the intervening period, from when the pictures were taken, there has been much infilling along the streets, perhaps best illustrated in the view of Westgate on page 35. The area on the right, once the site of Clarell Hall is empty, but now covered with housing. Many surrounding fields have also been built upon. Elsewhere in the village, a few of the old labourers' cottages have been demolished, though those on Victoria Terrace, since being 'modernised', have become rather desirable and sought after residences, commanding high prices. How the old labourers would have marvelled at the latter fact were they around today. Some of the more recent photgraphs in this section and in the book as a whole, show a number of buildings in Wadworth prior to demolition in the 1960s, when the area witnessed much house building. Wadworth's Main Street, in line with the rise in traffic, has also been widened.

In the business section, one of the only shops still thriving today is the one at Bawtry carrying the name of Frost. Tickhill butcher Thomas Woodcock is captured proudly posing, along with his family, outside his shop against a background of meat. With the current stringent health regulations and the BSE scare that is a sight which, surely, will never be witnessed again. How times have changed! Neither too I suspect will we see a hay and straw dealer posing as proud as W. Turner on page 64.

To my mind, the events section is where Scrivens and Crossland really show their skills as photographers, producing some really charming pictures. Scrivens took the ones of the bicycle gymkhana at Bawtry Hall and Mrs Peake (of Bawtry Hall) at the garden fete of 1908. In turn, Crossland painstakingly recorded the erection of the Tickhill public library and the cutting of the railway through the area, along with the construction of the railway station. How well the workmen and navvies appear to have coped using their extremely limited resources and primitive equipment.

Clearly, with the advent of motorised traffic an event like the Wadworth Feast and Maypole celebrations could not take place in the centre of the village ever again.

In the group of pictures of buildings, we may note that all three areas contained large houses: Bawtry Hall, Tickhill Castle and Wadworth Hall. Thankfully, all three still survive intact today, which is more than can be said for the once splendid houses and mansions in other parts of the Doncaster area. Most of the pubs depicted still survive too, albeit in a much altered form, catering for modern tastes. The aerial views, mostly taken from church towers, will provide an opportunity for people to check which buildings are now missing, besides observing how certain vistas appeared in former times.

I am pleased with range of pictures included and hope the reader has many happy hours looking at them.

One
Rambling Round

Feeding the ducks at Tickhill, looking along Dam Road, where Rowland Bridge House can be seen in the distance.

Children at Bawtry Market Cross, which possibly dates from the eighteenth century.

Delivery lads proudly pose outside H.J. Willows' supply stores which sold confectionery and groceries in the High Street, Bawtry. Is the gentleman with the moustache, who can just be seen standing in the doorway, H.J. Willows himself? Judging by the shop window display on the right, the picture must have been taken at Easter.

Another, later view, of the same shop depicted above, but this time it has different tenants, with H.J. Willows' name no longer displayed. Note how the shop appears to have different floor levels, one half being three storey, while the other part is only two. The entrance to Swan Street can just be seen on the right.

Two views of South Parade, Bawtry, showing what is traditionally known as the first house in Yorkshire, or No. 1 Yorkshire, when entering the area from the south. The three storey building, which is presently No. 2 South Parade, dates from the early nineteenth century. It is an attractive building with a central doorway displaying a Doric pillar surround. Beyond that house and seen in the picture above, are two, attractive, double-fronted properties, dating from the same period, with a central carriageway entrance. At one time, the properties along South Parade were occupied by professional people and those of independent means.

Wharf Street, Bawtry, looking towards High Street and Scot Lane. The Wharf Street name reminds us of the time when the town was an inland port on the River Idle. Dutch House, the three storey building on the left at the junction with Church Street, contains, hidden in the ivy, a Dutch gable dating from around 1690. The three storey property with bow windows further along the throughfare is Leigh House, dating from around 1800.

South Parade Bawtry, looking north.

Two views depicting Bawtry Market Place. John Walker states in one of the signs that his garage is, 'The Original Bawtry Garage. Established in 1906. Eight Years Before Any Other'. From the other signs we can also learn that he undertook general engineering and machine work, acetylene welding and decarbonizing. The 'up-to-date' workshops at the rear could accommodate twenty-five cars.

Gainsborough Road at Church Street corner, Bawtry, looking towards the South Parade and High Street junction, where Bawtry Hall is visible beyond. The Ship Inn is on the right.

The Town or Public Hall, Market Place, Bawtry, the date on the frontage clearly indicating when it was erected. It had cost £1,100 to build, and could hold 450 people, being let at the time for all kinds of entertainments. The building also contained a reading room and was well supplied with daily, monthly and weekly papers and periodicals. It later became the Bawtry Working Men's Club and Institute.

Views along Swan Street, Bawtry. The thoroughfare contains a number of splendid late eighteenth and early nineteenth century three storey properties.

A row of shops on High Street, Bawtry, featuring Baines' cafe and the premises of J.H. Herring, family grocer and provisions merchant, who patriotically displays a Union Jack. The signs indicate that Baines opened on Sunday and that Herring was also a dealer in offal. The three storey, bay windowed property, just off centre, was at one time the Old House Hotel, the building dating from around 1805. The other building of a similar height, to the left, was also erected about the same time.

Market Place, Bawtry, showing the Bawtry Working Men's Club and Institute, formerly the Town Hall, erected in 1890. The fish stall of T. and E. Bailey is to the left. On the opposite side the property dated from the seventeenth century, but has since been demolished. Moving along, the building with a central carriageway arch once housed the Angel Inn, closing in 1907. Adjoining it, with the gable end facing the street, is the old hospital of St Mary Magdalene.

High Street, Bawtry, looking east. The Marquis of Granby, now named simply The Granby, dates from the late eighteenth century and is pictured on the right, at the time when it was owned by Wath based brewers Whitworth, Son and Nephew.

High Street, Bawtry, looking east, when the problems of traffic congestion and finding a place to park were nothing like they are today. Also at that time, Willows' old property, already seen on page 11, was occupied by the Doncaster Mutual Co-operative.

Top Street, Bawtry, facing north, linking Tickhill Road and Doncaster Road. The property on the left, partially hidden by bushes, is the three storeyed Harworth House which dates from the eighteenth century. The row of cottages on the right, Nos 15-19 Top Street, was erected during the early nineteenth century.

Doncaster Road, Bawtry, looking from the junction with Top Street towards the High Street. Left of the telegraph pole the quaint row of cottages, numbered 3-11 School Hill, was built between 1820 and 1830. To the right, Bawtry Free School was erected in 1821-22 and extended in 1888. The school's front entrance features a triangular typanum, supported on two Tuscan columns.

South Parade, Bawtry, looking north. The building housing the garage has since been demolished.

South Parade, Bawtry, facing south; Gainsborough Road is on the left. One of the properties left of the central telegraph pole houses the Palace Cinema, which opened just after the First World War, closing around 1961. The building has since been demolished.

Doncaster Road, Bawtry. The farm house on the left dates from about 1825. The Methodist chapel is on the right and, today, is a visible reminder of the standing and influence of Wesleyan Methodism at the outset of the present century. Left of the church is a pinfold, once used for holding stray animals.

High Street, Bawtry, looking towards the Wesleyan chapel, which replaced an earlier nineteenth century structure situated in Church Walk. The new chapel opened in June 1903, at a cost of £2,700, and seated 500.

Doncaster Road and Great North Road looking south. It's difficult to imagine now that this was once the main road between London and Edinburgh, along which stage coaches passed.

Doncaster Road and Great North Road looking north. The cottage on the right has since been demolished.

A view along St Martin's Avenue with a gated, private road. The properties, which include bungalows, semi-detached and detached houses, were built during the 1920s. Among the first residents were local business folk and professionals.

The corner of Church Street and Swan Street, with hairdresser Miles Smith prominently displaying his barber's pole. The row of brick-built, pantiled cottages dates from the early nineteenth century.

Church Street, facing north, with plumbers Marrison and Sons' premises on the right. The three storey building on the left is Wharf House.

Church Street, Bawtry. The church of St Nicholas is made of stone and was built partly in the Norman style, consisting of nave, aisles and a western tower with pinnacles. Formerly a chapelry of the Benedictine Priory of Blyth, a prominent feature of the church is the twelfth century doorway on the northern side. The main structure dates from the thirteenth or fourteenth centuries and the tower was largely rebuilt in 1712 and 1713. The church was repaired in 1839, restored in 1901, and can accommodate 300 people. The register dates from 1653.

Church Street, Bawtry, looking towards Gainsborough Road, from Cockhill Close. The row of cottages on the left, numbered 80-90, was erected around 1820.

Church Street, Bawtry. This picture is worth comparing with a similar view on page 24, noting the alterations which have occurred.

Scene at Bawtry's Church Street and Swan Street junction, looking towards the church, with William Ainley's grocery and bakery shop on the right. The three storey property beyond the shop was formerly a chapel.

Church Street, Bawtry, facing Gainsborough Road.

The Parade, High Street, Bawtry, which includes at least three cafes, a hairdressers and a garage. Clearly this was to cater for the advent of motorised traffic passing through the town on the Great North Road. Bawtry had experienced a decline in trade since the coaching days but in addition to the Great North Road, it has been said that the effect of the opening of Boothferry Bridge in 1929, increased traffic overnight through the town.

Baines' cafe and confectionery shop, High Street, Bawtry, clearly announcing that teas and luncheons could be obtained on the premises. Are the people proudly posing for the camera in the doorway members of the Baines' family?

High Street, Bawtry, during the onset of motorised traffic. Sydney Barton's garage, off centre to the right, is accommodated in a former three storey town house built around 1800. There is a 1677 date stone and monogram on the frontage, the origins of which are unknown.

High Street, Bawtry, showing a collection of properties and traders including G.F. Marrison & Sons, building contractors, the Old House Hotel and Marsden's Bawtry Chocolate Box.

Station Road, Bawtry, along which groups of houses were built before and after the First World War.

Station Road, Bawtry, looking towards the Station Hotel. Nearfield House is the first property on the left, dating from around 1810. It has since undergone drastic alterations, as have the adjacent premises numbered 31-35, which were erected about the same period.

Station Road, Bawtry, looking east, with the Station Hotel off centre to the right. The impressive row of four terraced houses on the left, numbered 85-91, was constructed during the late nineteenth century.

South Parade, Bawtry, facing south, on 24 April 1908 after an apparently late fall of snow. The gates on the right lead to Bawtry Hall, at that time occupied by Captain George Herbert Peake, JP.

A postcard view of Castlegate, Tickhill, looking north, illustrating how tightly grouped together the properties are. The postmark on the back of the postcard is 17 October 1904. Note the bow windows in the property on the right.

Castlegate, looking towards West Gate and the old Millstone Inn. The picture pre-dates the latter property being rebuilt in 1908. Depicted on the right are the premises of painter and paper-hanger J.W. Hill; his sign announces that estimates 'are free'.

Castlegate, Tickhill, facing north. It is thought that the street may once have accommodated a market area.

A group of cottages on the eastern side of Castlegate. The limestone cottages on the left include Yorkshire sliding sash windows.

View along Castlegate, Tickhill, looking towards the Castle, with the Co-op on the right.

View across the Mill Dam, Tickhill, showing the Corn Mill on the right.

Westgate, facing west, with the Travellers Rest beer house on the right. In 1907, when William Hancock was the landlord, the premises were altered and a new extension built. Note the steps leading up to the cottage doorways.

The western end of Westgate, *c.*1905. The old section of the Travellers Rest is on the right. Also visible on the left is the old junction with Worksop Road and Maltby Road. At the corner of the latter were once St Mary's Bridge and a bleach yard.

Westgate, looking west, with the Millstone Inn on the left and the Carpenters Arms on the right. The Millstone Inn, dating from at least 1803, was rebuilt in 1908 by Mappin's Masborough Old Brewery Ltd. Much building work took place at the eastern end of the thoroughfare during the first half of the nineteenth century.

Westgate, before many houses had been infilled on the northern side during the present century. Clarel Hall once existed on the area of land to the right.

A section of property on Westgate, Tickhill.

A row of houses on the eastern side of Rawson Road, Tickhill. Council houses were built on the western side during the 1920s.

View of the Mill Dam, Tickhill, looking towards the Millstone Inn and Castle Gate.

View across the Mill Dam, Tickhill. The Corn Mill is shown in the centre.

Victoria Terrace in St Mary's Road, Tickhill, looking north. The ten limestone ashlar and pantile cottages that make up the terrace date from around 1840. Victoria Terrace was formerly titled 'Shepherd's Row'.

Mangham Lane, Tickhill. The thoroughfare was once titled Blanch Lane and formerly accommodated a Methodist chapel.

Northgate, Tickhill, facing north. The Royal Oak public house can be indentified within the group of buildings.

Northgate, Tickhill, looking towards the Buttercross.

Doncaster Road, Tickhill, facing north, *c.* 1907. Note the row of five brick cottages known locally as Shaw's Cottages, Shaw's Row or even White Scraper's Row, due to the white painted boot and shoe scrapers by the front doors. These cottages were later demolished to make way for Whinnery Close.

Doncaster Road, looking south, showing in the left foreground the 'opening-up' of a plot of land in preparation for the building of a row of seven small terraced houses for H. Duckenfield. The plans were passed in January 1911 and the houses were built and ready for occupation by September of that year. The terrace was named Prospect View.

Doncaster Road, Tickhill, with Jarvis & Son's confectionery and provisions store featured on the left.

)oncaster Road, Tickhill, facing north.

Looking along Castlegate, Tickhill, from the Market Place, *c.* 1912. Note the Market Cross built in 1776, the post office, public library, the gas lamp post and tree-covered castle mound.

It has been suggested that the original Market Cross at Tickhill was situated at the junction c Wellingley Lane and Doncaster Road. A 1724 estate map may indicate that possibility. A plaque on the east-facing side of the present cross reveals that it was constructed in 1777, an renovated in 1898. Also situated on the site are three Victorian troughs and a water pump.

View along St Mary's Gate, Tickhill, probably taken from a first floor room of photographer George Crossland's house.

Pinfold Lane, Tickhill, looking towards St Mary's church.

View along Lindrick, Tickhill, with Bower's Walk leading off to Westgate on the right and Water Lane to the left. Bower's Walk takes its name from Henry Bower, the one time owner of Westfield Farm, later named Westgarth.

Tickhill Spital, east of the village, looking towards Hesley with Rossington beyond. A medieva hospital was formerly situated at the Spital, being noted in 1325 for brethren, priests anc servants.

Sunderland Street, Tickhill, with the White Horse public house on the left and the Scarborough Arms beyond. The Gleadall family held the licence for the White Horse for a number of years until it closed as a beer house in 1907.

New Road, Tickhill, linking Pinfold Lane and St Mary's Road, was constructed in 1867 at a cost of £900.

Row of houses, in Castlegate, Tickhill. The property with the badge above the front door was occupied by the local policeman.

People in Tickhill Castle grounds after a local hunt meet. The Castle is situated south east of the town centre being owned by the Queen in right of her Duchy of Lancaster.

Northgate, Tickhill, facing north.

Northgate, Tickhill, featuring the Three Crowns public house and St Leonard's. The façade of the latter building dates from 1470, being restored in 1851. It presently serves as the parish room for St Mary's church.

A view looking across the Friary Field, Tickhill, towards Maltby Road, showing a group of old cottages. The picture must have been taken around 1905 as the old Travellers Rest beer house can still be seen, prior to alterations.

View of Tickhill from Limestone Hill.

Street scene at Wadworth. Many of the village's streets are now unrecognisable from former times, with much new house building taking place.

Main Street, Wadworth, showing the maypole. The Fox & Hounds Inn, advertising Whitworth's ales, was considerably altered in subsequent years, as can be seen in a view on page 51.

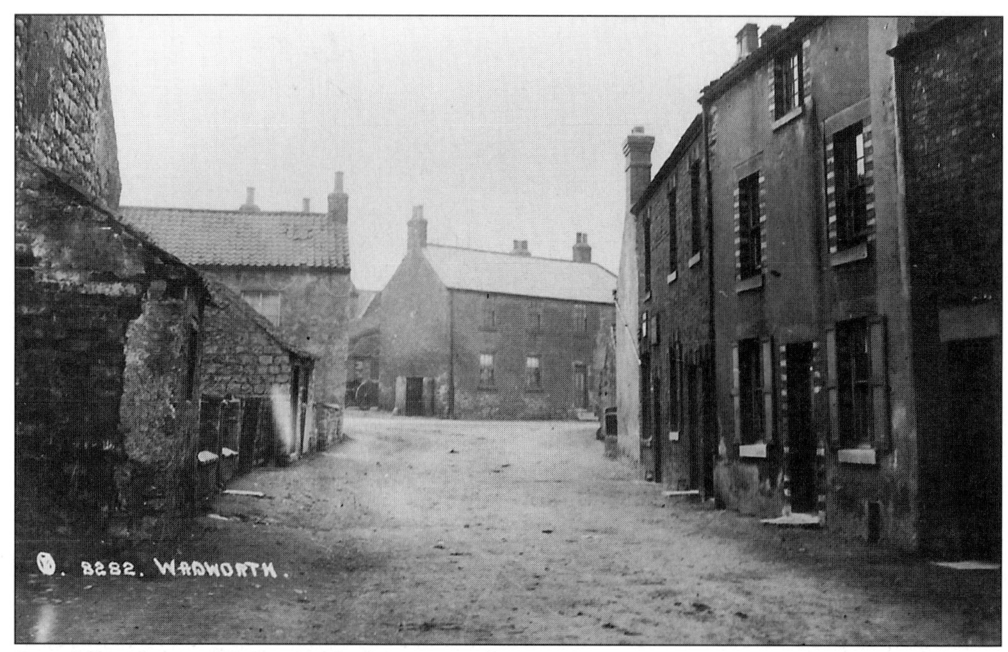

Post Office Street, Wadworth, looking towards Main Street.

Post Office Row, Wadworth. Note the Wesleyan chapel in the background.

Properties situated along Ratten Row, Wadworth, photographed during the 1960s, before being demolished.

Main Street, Wadworth, probably during the 1930s when the Fox & Hounds Inn, on the left, was undergoing extensive alterations.

House situated on Ratten Row, Wadworth. The property has since been demolished.

Properties at the junction of Walnut Tree Hill and Ratten Row, Wadworth.

Two
Commerce

Sydney Barton standing outside his garage on High Street, Bawtry.

Womack & Sons, North Road Garage and provisions shop, High Street, Bawtry. Mr Womack is pictured in the shop doorway.

Womack's Garage, Bawtry, with Scot Lane on the left.

Womack's Garage, High Street, Bawtry.

Womack's Garage, High Street, Bawtry.

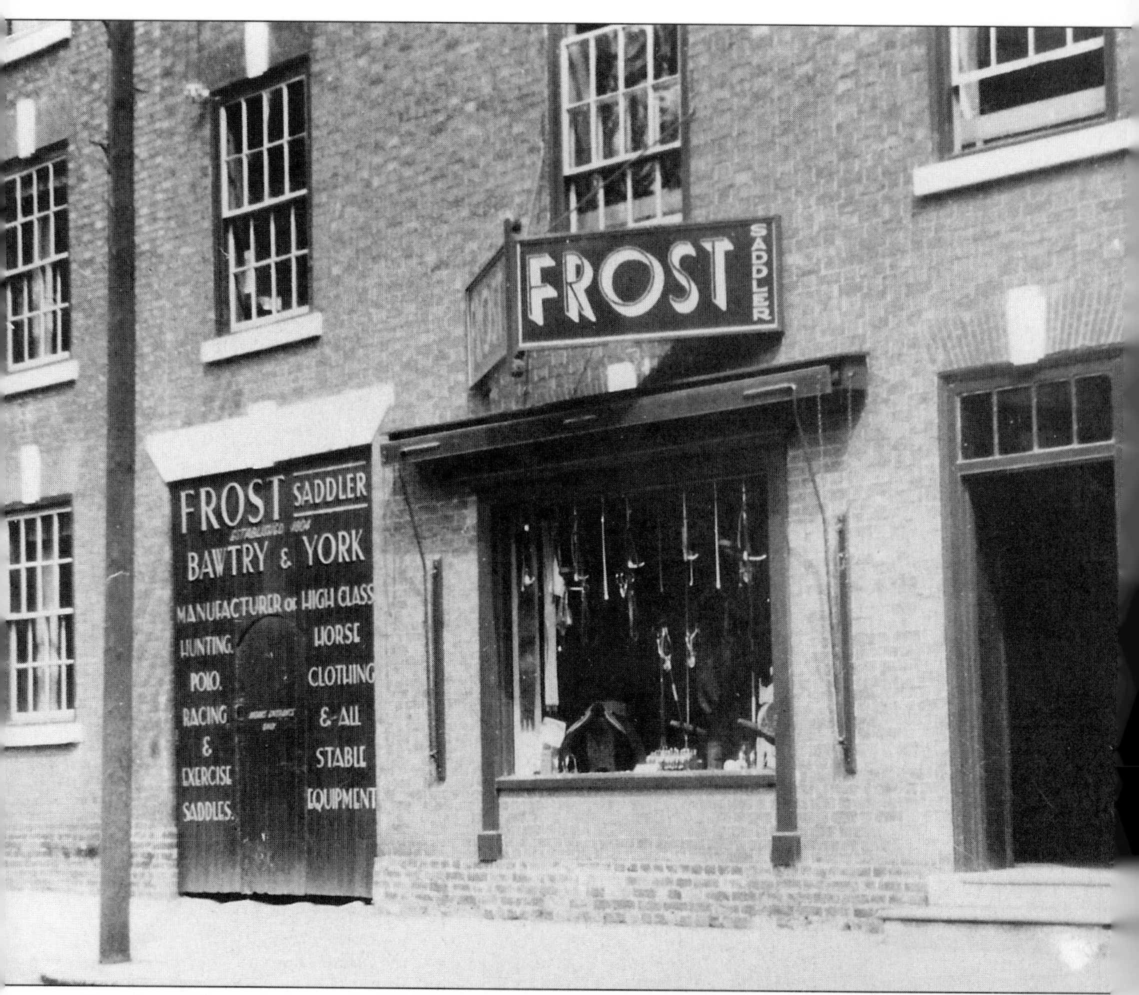

Frost's saddlers shop on South Parade, Bawtry. The sign informs us that the business, with another outlet in York, has been established since 1804 and that the type of work undertaken includes the manufacture of high class hunting, polo, racing and exercise saddles. Frost could also supply horse clothing and all stable equipment.

Grocer and ironmonger W. Colbeck's shop, at the corner of Castlegate and St Mary's Gate, Tickhill.

Thomas Woodcock's butchers shop, Market Place, Tickhill. Posing for the photographer from left to right are: -?-, Tom Brown (butcher's assistant), Gladys Eaton, Thomas Woodcock, Mrs Woodcock, Rene Woodcock, Elsie Eaton, -?-. The picture was taken before June 1910 when alterations were made to the premises. The shop is currently occupied by D.J. Fenton.

Jarvis & Sons' grocers shop, Market Place, Tickhill.

Jarvis & Sons' general drapers and outfitters shop, Sunderland Street, Tickhill.

George Crossland was born at Ecclesfield in 1861, arriving in Tickhill around the turn of the century from Mexborough, where he was an overseer and guardian. He took an active part in the community, becoming an organist and choirmaster; conductor of the Tickhill Choral Society; JP and Chairman of the Tickhill Urban District Council. He lived first at Rowland House, moved to Castlegate (his shop is pictured above), and spent his last years at Poplar Farm, where he died in 1930. Besides his public service and musical contributions, Tickhill will be forever in his debt for photographing numerous scenes and events in and around the area during a period of considerable development.

George Crossland's musical abilities and contributions were considerable. He was fond of music all his life. As a youth, he conducted a flute band and later played double bass in the Denaby Main String Band. He also played violin, cello and was organist and choirmaster at the Wesleyan Church at Tickhill. He once estimated that he had taught children and choirs at least 1,500 hymns and tunes.

George Crossland, his wife, their daughter Zillah and Mrs Chambers, George Crossland's mother-in-law. The photograph was probably taken in George Crossland's studio in Castlegate.

Jarvis & Sons' grocery shop, Market Place, Tickhill. Plans for alterations to the premises were approved by the WRCC and sealed by the TUDC on 8 May 1906. The new building was completed and opened by 1907. Two years later a new, model bakery was erected adjoining the premises at the rear.

Tickhill Post Office, situated at the corner of Sunderland Street and Castlegate since 1803. It had previously occupied a building adjacent to the Red Lion public house on the opposite side of the road.

William Turner, hay and straw dealer, whose business premises were in Sunderland Street. William is holding the horse's head. The woman is housemaid Miss Laura Newbound and she is conversing with William's driver, Ted Gleadall. The yard and buildings no longer exist.

The Doncaster Mutual Co-operative and Industrial Society's building in Castlegate, Tickhill. In 1912, A.C. Heywood's shop and an adjacent brick cottage were demolished to make way for the extensions to the original DMC & IS store. These were to become the butchers and drapers departments of the extended store, the original premises becoming the grocery department. This view shows the new store shortly after it was fully occupied in May 1913.

The rendered cottage seen here was the first to be demolished in order to build the original stores of the Doncaster Mutual Co-operative and Industrial Society Limited in Castlegate in 1909. It later became the grocery department of the Doncaster Co-operative Stores.

Butchers shop, Market Place, Tickhill.

Tickhill Garage, Castlegate. The garage was once owned by a Mr Preece; petrol pumps first appeared on his forecourt during the 1920s.

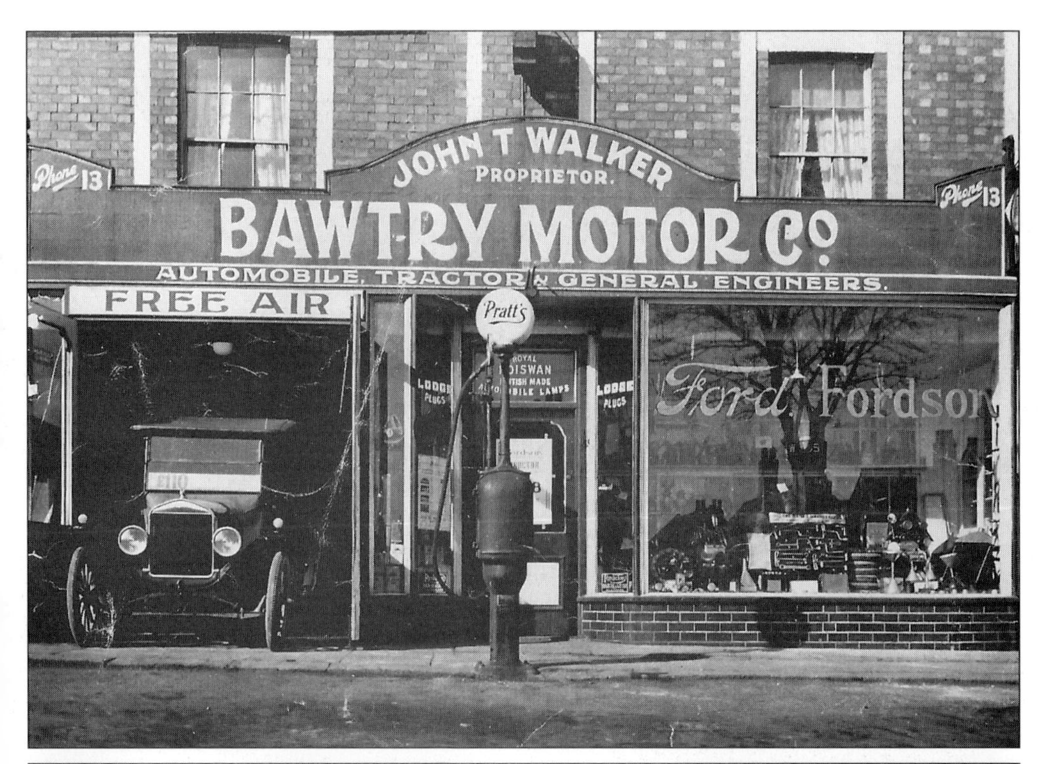

Exterior and interior views of J.T. Walker's Bawtry Motor Co.'s premises in Market Place, Bawtry.

According to his obituary in the *Doncaster Gazette* of 4 January 1962, John Thomas Walker started the business – now the Bawtry Motor Co. Ltd – about 1900. He originally dealt in cycles, then motorcycles, and eventually motor cars. The first petrol pump on the Great North Road was erected at his garage. Mr Walker sold the business in 1946. Mr Walker was a past chairman of Bawtry Parish Council, and for something like half-a-century served education in the Bawtry district. In 1957, he laid the foundation stone of the Mayflower School in Bawtry. A well-known Freemason, Mr Walker held provincial office in Lincolnshire. He was a past master of Isle of Axholme Lodge, Crowle, and the first master of Bawtry Lodge of which he was a founder. He resided in Scot Lane, Bawtry, dying aged 86, shortly before New Year's Eve in 1961.

Three
Events

Procession at the Tickhill Market Cross.

Bicycle gymkhana at Bawtry Hall garden fete on 12 August 1908. The fête was held in aid of the Bawtry and District Nursing Association.

Children in fancy dress at Bawtry Hall garden fete, 12 August 1908. The children's procession and dance and baby show was perhaps the most interesting and popular entertainment of the afternoon. In the former about fifty children drawn from Bawtry, Austerfield, Rossington and Newington, in handsome attire, formed up on the lawns straight in front of the mansion. The proceedings were enhanced by the music rendered by the Tickhill Brass Band and the entertainments by the South Parade Pierrotts.

The Fitzwilliam hounds in the Market Place, Bawtry.

Bawtry Coronation Cycle Parade held in June 1911.

Mrs Peake at Bawtry Hall garden fete on 12 August 1908. Mrs Peake was the eldest daughter of the Hon. John C. Dundas, brother of the first Marquess of Zetland. Mrs Peake helped her husband in his many philanthropic efforts, co-operating with him in supporting Boy Scouts, Girl Guides and Red Cross Organisations.

Mrs Peake was Hon Secretary of the North Notts musical tournament for many years. She helped train the Bawtry Parish Church choir, and instituted singing competitions at Bawtry. It was said that nearly every social project in the neighbourhood benefitted from her help. She died aged 72, at Sutton Hall, Thirsk, in 1945, having moved there following the sale of Bawtry Hall to the R.A.F. in 1939.

Two photographs giving an indication of the scenes encountered in Bawtry Market Place during the First World War.

Ship's rudder, passing through Bawtry, High Street, while heading south.

Scene in Bawtry Market Place during the First World War.

Station Road, Bawtry, welcomes the Queen. At one time, while visiting Doncaster Races, the Queen stayed with Lord Scarborough at Sandbeck Park, often alighting from the royal train at Bawtry Station. The above picture was perhaps taken on one of those occasions, revealing Bawtry's patriotic fervour.

The 'Fish Pond' was at the far end of a field behind Castle Folds Farm, adjacent to Tickhill Castle. Skating continued there until at least the outbreak of the Second World War.

Tickhill fire fighters preparing their primitive equipment. And, perhaps from the seemingly casual way the men are stocking up with water, they are only practising their duties.

In the Coronation Festivites booklet of 1911, the tableau depicted here was entitled Man of War. Utilizing Messrs R.H. Rawson & Sons' horse and dray, HMS *Empire*, with Beatrice Hancock as Britannia, was entered in the procession pageant commemorating the coronation of King George V and Queen Mary in June 1911. This photograph was taken in the grounds of Sandrock House, Tickhill.

Empire Day celebrations, Tickhill.

A scene in Northgate, June 1911, showing part of Tickhill's procession and pageant celebrating the coronation of King George V and Queen Mary.

Celebrations in Castlegate, Tickhill, facing the Castle mound, seen in the background. The celebrations were part of the town's procession and pageant for the 1911 Coronation.

In October 1906, the will of the late Henry Shaw made provision for the building of a public library and reading rooms in Tickhill. Matters were eventually completed between the executors of his will and the Urban District Council in May 1907 and in October of the same year, architect P.N. Brundell's plans for the library were accepted by the Council. In December, R.H. Rawson and Sons' tender of £1,267 to construct the library was accepted. This picture shows the site for the library prior to the existing building's demolition in January 1908. Although the sign above the doorway appears to read Joseph Fitzgerald, it is known that Joseph Denton, gas fitter, occupied a workshop and gas works at the rear of the premises.

Tickhill Public Library under construction in Castlegate, *c.* March 1908, with R.H. Rawson's workforce posing for the camera. G.H. Rawson and J. Rawson are the two gentlemen seen on the extreme right.

Probably taken in June 1908, this photograph shows the Tickhill Public Library, Castlegate, almost completed. It was agreed by the Urban District Council that a brass tablet would be mounted in the library as a memorial to the late Mr Henry Shaw, 'the donor of the site and building'.

The official opening of Tickhill Public Library and Reading Rooms by Lord Scarborough took place on Wednesday 7 October 1908 at 3.00 pm. Lord Scarborough's charabanc is seen outside the library. Note the fair wagon on the left, near the Cross.

A view of the Grove? Hounds Meet in the Market Place, Tickhill in 1912, viewed from Sunderland Street. Mr Robert Saxton, a local coach proprietor, is seen in the foreground, mounted on his hunter.

Tickhill Town Crier George Holden, in the cart, and Abner Rawson, standing, are pictured touring the area in 1921, promoting brothers Tom and Arthur Kirkland for the local elections.

The meet of the hounds at Tickhill Spital and Harworth Road. The date is unknown but the motorcycle in the foreground may provide a clue.

The meet of the hounds at Tickhill Spital. Rock House may be seen in the background.

The Doncaster Mutual Co-operative and Industrial Society Limited, Castlegate, Tickhill, under construction in 1909. Workmen standing on the girder are, left to right: J. Kimberley, T. Glasbey, J. Herrington, H. Stennett, W.H. Gleadall. Those below the girder are, left to right: C. Whinfrey, J. Mannifield. The two girders shown each weighed thirty-two hundredweight.

The meet of the hounds at Tickhill Spital and Harworth Road.

Tuby's fair at the Market Cross, Tickhill. On the attraction to the left are the words Olympic Games – probably a reference to the 1908 Olympic Games held in London. The picture is thought to have been taken in 1910.

Preparations being made for Tickhill Autumn Fair in 1913. The fair was held every October at the Cross, and during that period the North Gate and Sunderland Street junction was closed to traffic. Harnies' and Tuby's roundabouts are in evidence. Later, there would be Aunt Sally, hoop-la and darts stalls, plus other attractions. A fair was also held on August bank holiday Mondays.

Tickhill Show.

Early in 1913, a telegraph pole was erected outside Tickhill Post Office, at the Sunderland Street and Castlegate corner, immediately courting controversy because it was noted that it caused an obstruction to the footpath. As a safety precaution, wooden lathes were fixed around the lower section of the pole and painted a light colour, making it more noticeable, particularly at night.

The Goods Station buildings and the stationmaster's house under construction at Tickhill in 1906. When completed two years later, the station included two platforms with a main station building, a separate waiting room, an overbridge and a signal box, as well as four sidings.

The wrong caption has been given to this view as regular passenger services on the SYJR did not commence until 1 December 1910. This photograph shows an inspection train or a directors' special and was taken at Wadworth and Tickhill Railway Station on 16 September 1908. The railway companies responsible for the construction of this line included the Midland, Great Central, North Eastern, Lancashire and Yorkshire and Great Northern, together forming the South Yorkshire Joint Railway Board.

View of Tickhill Station and signal box from the lineside. The picture was probably taken around 1908, shortly after the railway was operational. The platform was 350 ft in length and there was double track through the station.

At 7.30 am on 6 July 1910, the first trip from Tickhill Station ran to Grimsby Docks and Cleethorpes. The Tickhill Wesleyan Sunday School went on the trip and included 142 adults and 122 children. The train is seen here prior to departure.

The first trip from Tickhill Station on 6 July 1910. Later, for a period at least, there were four passenger services each day between Doncaster and Worksop, the journey taking, on average, fifty-four minutes.

First trip from Tickhill Station, 6 July 1910. Passenger services were withdrawn in 1929, with goods and a few excursion trains continuing until October, 1964.

A view of the South Yorkshire Joint Railway temporary road bridge at Tickhill and Wadworth Station, taken on 23 September 1906. A brick-built bridge was completed by August 1907.

Navvies pause for the photographer while working on the temporary road bridge over the South Yorkshire Joint Railway at Wadworth Bar, near the site of the Tickhill and Wadworth Railway Station.

Workmen posing, *c.* 1905, during the construction of one of the South Yorkshire Joint Railway Co.'s cuttings through either Apy Hill or All Hallows Hill, Tickhill. The joint line was constructed by the Leeds firm of Whittaker Brothers, with many Irish navvies being employed. The line was commenced from the Dinnington end, in November 1905 and completed, at Kirk Sandall, in August 1908.

Navvies pose for the camera alongside a steam-operated excavator and crane and horse-drawn tipper wagon in a cutting on the South Yorkshire Joint Railway at Hindley Closes, Tickhill. Apy Hill Lane bridge is in the background. The cutting was in the process of being widened around 1906.

Sinking for water at Wellingley, near Tickhill.

Celebrations near the Tickhill Market Cross, for the Relief of Maefeking.

Scene at the rear of butcher William Tiplady's premises in Castlegate, Tickhill, with a beast reputedly weighing 96 st 4 lbs.

The May Queen at Tickhill Buttercross.

May Queen celebrations near Tickhill Buttercross. Ena Harden was the May Queen. The tall girl on the right is Hilda Clarkson.

Floods in Castlegate, Tickhill, with the Co-op premises on the left.

Hunt meet at Wadworth.

Feast celebrations in 1912, in Wadworth Main Street.

On 25 April 1924 a *Doncaster Gazette* reporter asked: 'How long has there been a Maypole at Wadworth?' For the most part, the people in the village were agreed upon one thing: there has been one standing near the 'White Hart' ever since they can remember, ever since their fathers can remember. Perhaps a 100 years, perhaps longer was as far as they would commit themselves. One fascinating theory was suggested to the *Gazette* man endeavouring to obtain a little information about Wadworth and its maypole. 'Celebration Day' – the day when the pole was dressed – was on 29 May, Royal Oak Day, the day when Charles II entered London, in 1660, amid general rejoicing, as King. 'What more natural than that the good folk of Wadworth should erect a maypole as an indication that they were once more allowed to enjoy themselves?' That may have been the case. But, there is one thing which makes it improbable. The date of the celebration has, an old resident stated, been altered. It was originally earlier in the month, but on one occasion the day happened to be wet, and the festivities were postponed until 29 May. The reason that the date was kept in preference to the other was presumably that there was more chance of it being fine. The festivities usually opened with a tea. And after that there was the dressing of the pole with garlands, usually ten in number. The materials – cloth of varying colours – were purchased with money collected by the women folk, who sometimes carried the garlands round the village on a long pole, to the great delight of the inhabitants. Finally there was dancing and merry-making.

Interestingly, on 11 May 1950 the *Doncaster Chronicle* reported that Wadworth people were erecting the fourth Maypole in 57 years: 'The first of the four was blown down in a gale 57 years ago, its successor rotted and in 1923 the last pole was put in its place. It was brought all the way from Norway, via Hull and Tickhill and then by horse and cart to Wadworth, all for a cost of £17 10s. It was erected by voluntary labour. The new one came in a fashion and at a price to be expected in this modern age by motor lorry from Lincoln and was erected by a contractor for a cost of £45'.

Four

Buildings

The Three Crowns Inn before major alterations and additions took place between 1901 and 1902. It is interesting to note that H. Law, cycle repairer, also operated from part of the same premises. The parish rooms are also visible. Before alterations in 1851, the parish rooms were cottages with three sets of steps and three entrance doors at the front.

Much of the present Bawtry Hall was built following the sale in 1779 of Bawtry Manor to prominent West Yorkshire politician Pemberton Milnes of Wakefield. Following Milnes' death in 1795, his daughter Bridget inherited the Bawtry estate. When she died in 1835, the Hall's principal residents during the remainder of the century included Robert Pemberton Milnes, nephew of Pemberton Milnes and MP for Pontefract. The most noted occupant during the present century, and indeed the last private owner of Bawtry Hall, was Major George Herbert Peake, who purchased the property in 1904 from the Earl of Crewe. He added a wing to the Hall at the rear around 1905, incorporating a water tower. Major and Mrs Peake vacated the Hall at the outbreak of the Second World War. The Hall was then occupied by the R.A.F. until the 1980s.

Bawtry Hall.

Meet of the Fitzwilliam hounds in Bawtry Market Place, 15 March 1909. The photograph shows Mr and Mrs Peake of Bawtry Hall.

The painters and decorators of Doncaster firm, Postlethwaite and Stacey, are seen posing in front of Bawtry Hall.

Two views of the former GNR main line station at Bawtry, which closed on 6 October 1958.

Wesleyan Methodist chapel, Northgate, Tickhill. The original chapel was built on the corner of Bland Lane and Back Lane, (now Mangham Lane and St Mary's Road). Within twenty years the building was found to be too small so the chapel, pictured above, seating about 500 people, was built on a site in Northgate in 1837. The building was lowered and re-constructed between October 1961 and October 1963, providing more compact premises.

St Leonard's House, Northgate, Tickhill. The property was demolished in recent years, making way for a private housing development.

It has been assumed that St Mary's church, Tickhill replaced the earlier All Hallows church, serving smaller settlements, situated west of the road between Wilsic and Tickhill. There is no doubt that the present Tickhill church is a very impressive structure; some parts, including the western door, lower sections of the tower and chancel, date from the thirteenth century. Much of the rest betrays the influence of the perpendicular style, the work being carried out during the late fourteenth and early fifteenth century.

Sandrock House, Tickhill with a verandah built across to the sandstone rock. Sandrock House was extended by Benjamin H. Brooksbank in late 1907 and early 1908 from a small cottage. The 'old cottage' forms the kitchen end of the building. During the Second World War some officers from the Royal Artillery Corps were billeted at Sandrock.

Tickhill Castle Gateway, clearly visible from the road, and possibly dating from the 1100s, contains some of the earliest stonework to be found in the area. It has an upper storey, arguably built in the Tudor period with an impressive fireplace on the south wall. The groove for the portcullis and position of the gates can still be detected.

Tickhill Station in ruins, 25 April 1982. The building has since been demolished.

The Old National School Tickhill, situated within the church yard, but now demolished, being replaced by another building in Back Lane, now St Mary's Road. The gent leaning on the tombstone is thought to be 'Ratty' Beat, a local grave digger and rat catcher.

An Augustinian Friary was established, west of Tickhill Castle, in 1260 by the Clarel family. By the fourteenth century, around twenty-four friars lived at the friary. Yet by the dissolution of the monasteries in 1538, the numbers had waned to eight. The present house, seen here, is a former barn, containing a thirteenth century lancet window and other masonry from the original friary. There is also a thirteenth century archway with dog tooth decoration in the garden.

Wadworth Manor House, dating from around the late seventeenth century and containing mullioned widows. It is amongst the village's more important buildings, being restored during the early 1970s.

Wadworth Hall was built about 1749 to the designs of renowned architect James Paine for the Wordsworth family. In 1740/41, Paine had designed the interior decorations of Nostell Priory, and in 1744 had won the commission for the Doncaster Mansion House. Wadworth Hall is on the site of an earlier Elizabethan or Jacobean house, once occupied by the Copley family. The present Hall had a number of owners during the nineteenth and twentieth centuries and for some time, after being purchased by the West Riding County Council in 1957, was used as a Welfare Home for Aged Persons.

Wadworth Post Office, on Low Street. The property has since been demolished, the Post Office having moved to Main Street.

Five

Pubs

Millstone Inn, Westgate, Tickhill. The inn was formerly owned by Sheffield brewer John Newton Mappin.

References to the Black Bull, High Street, Bawtry, can be traced back to at least 1784, though the inn appears to have ceased trading sometime around 1881.

The Crown Inn, High Street, Bawtry, dating from at least 1772, was formerly an important posting and coaching house on the Great North Road. Its former owners include Lord Houghton, the New Trent Brewery Co. Ltd and the Barnsley Brewery Co. Ltd.

The Ship Inn, at the corner of Church Street and Gainsborough Road, and dating back to at least 1788, was rebuilt by Grimsby-based brewers Hewitt Bros in 1908.

The White Hart Inn on Swan Street, Bawtry, rebuilt around the turn of the century, survived a threat of closure by magistrates on the grounds of redundancy in 1937. Its former owners include Jane Fisher and Warwicks & Richardsons.

The Millstone Inn, Westgate, Tickhill. These two pictures show the premises before and after rebuilding. The new premises are a perfect example of what has become known in architectural terms as 'brewers' Tudor'. The old photograph was taken when Godfrey Emerson was the licensee. The inn can be dated back to at least 1803.

Station Hotel, Station Road, Bawtry, dating back to at least 1861. Past owners include Lord Houghton and the Worksop and Retford Brewery Co. Ltd. The premises were rebuilt in 1905.

Is this a Red Lion outing or is it a party of people from elsewhere 'halting for refreshments at Tickhill', as the caption states? Whatever, the probable destination of the excursion would have been Roche Abbey. The premises housing the shop of T. Guest, confectioner, to the left were, in the late 1870s, Mr and Mrs Beecham's private school.

Red Lion, Market Place, Tickhill. References to the Red Lion extend back to 1790. The inn has recently been re-named.

The Carpenters Arms, Westgate, Tickhill, dates from as early as 1822. Former owners include Slinn Searle & Co Ltd and Whitworth, Son & Nephew Ltd.

The Travellers Rest, Westgate, Tickhill, dates back as a beer house to at least 1851 when Innocent Wakinson was the occupant. On 8 March 1907, it was announced in the *Doncaster Chronicle* that William Hancock had occupied the premises for thirty-five years and owned them for thirty-seven years. A year later the premises were rebuilt. In 1927 brewers Hewitt Bros bought the Traveller's Rest for £6,100 from the estate of Jane Hancock, deceased. The premises gained a full licence in 1949.

The Royal Oak in Northgate, Tickhill began as a beer house dating back to at least 1869, when it was occupied by the Green family, members of which are pictured above. Brewers Tennant Bros acquired the property from Vernon Green in 1950.

Fox & Hounds, Main Street, Wadworth, the history of which dates back to at least 1835. Prior to this date the pub may have been known as the Angel. At one time the Fox & Hounds belonged to Nicholson Brothers' Conisborough brewery and the premises were considerably altered around 1935, after a threat to revoke the license was overturned. The licensee at the time the picture was taken was W. Haslam.

Fox & Hounds Inn, Main Street, Wadworth, pictured after being altered.

Six
Formal Groups

Children posing outside the Public Library, Castlegate, Tickhill.

Children at the new National School, Tickhill.

Staff at Tickhill Station. The stationmaster, Charles England, is seated in the centre.

Outing from the Carpenters Arms on 23 June 1913. References to the pub date back to 1822, with the Hancock family holding the licence for at least fifty years during the nineteenth century. Past brewery owners have included Slinn Searle and Co. Ltd, and Whitworth, Son and Nephew Ltd.

Agricultural scene at Tickhill, probably taken sometime during the First World War, judging by the presence of the soldiers.

Soldiers at Tickhill during the First World War. Two cavalry regiments trained in the village during the period of hostilities, with a number of public buildings being commandeered for their use.

Soldiers at Tickhill during the First World War, undertaking blacksmith's work in one of the village's long yards. Forty Tickhill men lost their lives in that war; a memorial was erected and unveiled for them in the churchyard during 1920.

Tickhill school group.

Tickhill Thursday Cricket Club. Initially, around 1850, Tickhill cricket matches were played on a ground in Water Lane, but twenty years later the present site off Sunderland Street was adopted.

Tickhill campanologists, from left to right: ? Jenkinson, Frank Jenkinson, Tommy Mannifield, ? Hackford, ? Ellis, Charlie Ainley, -?-.

Women who have made garlands for the Wadworth Maypole celebrations are pictured outside the White Hart Inn on Main Street.

A posed postcard view on the steps of Tickhill Buttercross, 'after school hours'. Which class was it? Whose chair was it? What year was it? All these questions spring to mind while looking at the picture.

Children posing with Wadworth church in the background.

Employees of Tickhill builder J.H. Rawson on a day trip to Welbeck Abbey.

Seven

Aerial Views

View from the top of Wadworth church.

Aerial view of Bawtry. The Crown Hotel is just off centre to the right.

View from Tickhill church looking down on St Mary's Road.

View from the top of Wadworth church. Doncaster Road is on the left.

View from the top of Tickhill church, looking towards the Buttercross.

Acknowledgements

I would like to thank my good friend Ken Kimberley
for his invaluable help whilst I was compling information on the Tickhill pictures.
Gratitude should also be expressed to the following people:
Trevor and Lynne Lee, Mary Read, and Peter Womack.